March 2018
great to be together!
" older people, deeper love "
your sis

UNCONDITIONAL

UNCONDITIONAL

OLDER DOGS, DEEPER LOVE

JANE SOBEL KLONSKY

NATIONAL GEOGRAPHIC

Washington, D.C.

Since 1888, the National Geographic Society has funded more than 12,000 research, exploration, and preservation projects around the world. National Geographic Partners distributes a portion of the funds it receives from your purchase to National Geographic Society to support programs including the conservation of animals and their habitats.

National Geographic Partners
1145 17th Street NW
Washington, DC 20036-4688 USA

Become a member of National Geographic and activate your benefits today at natgeo.com/jointoday.

For information about special discounts for bulk purchases, please contact National Geographic Books Special Sales: ngspecsales@ngs.org

For rights or permissions inquiries, please contact National Geographic Books Subsidiary Rights: BookRights@natgeo.com

Additional photography: 12–13, Lisa Cueman; 14–15, Kacey Klonsky; 15, Gwenn Bogart

ISBN: 978-1-4262-1711-1

Printed in China

16/RRDS/1

This book is dedicated to all the beloved dogs who have left us but are still in our hearts and remain with us in spirit. And to my sweet dogs, Charlie and Sam, who remind me every day why I love this project.

Claire, 16 years (Debbie Marks)
Page 1: Hope, 11 years (Teri Hembree)
Pages 2–3: Kim Pieper and Chloe, 14 years

CONTENTS

INTRODUCTION

Throughout my 38 years as a professional photographer, I've dreamed of creating a body of work around my passion for dogs. It was a chance encounter with a senior English Bulldog named Clementine that made my dream a reality.

It started with the endearing sight of Clemmie happily lying on a comfy bed next to the desk of my insurance broker, Angela. What piqued my interest was their close connection, evident in their interactions. Clemmie was nine years old, and being with Angela was clearly her reason for existence. There was an inexplicable depth to the bond between them. I felt compelled to capture it, so I arranged to photograph Clemmie and Angela the next day.

This first photo shoot with Clementine awakened something in me: a longing to capture the remarkable relationships between people and their dogs in the twilight of their lives. It stirred so many emotions within me, from excitement to satisfaction, as well as an awareness of the privilege of capturing such intimate relationships. From there, the project took off. I found that people with older dogs truly wanted to engage with me—and were happy to spend hours on photo shoots! When I shared their stories with my husband, Arthur, he suggested that the participants contribute their stories. As I began to collect the personal narratives, I realized that the stories brought a depth to the photos that I hadn't anticipated. The poignancy of these sentiments added immeasurably to what became Project Unconditional.

I've always looked at my work as a celebration of relationships, capturing these amazing bonds of unconditional love and loyalty. It's a feeling that was articulated beautifully by John Maggiotto, when he wrote about his old friend Stella, a 15-year-old Labrador Retriever. "I never liked her in a collar. It made us more equal if she stayed with me by choice. Our favorite game was to play hide-and-seek on our walks. We still walk the same route, but with more patience. She's a smart one: She no longer searches; she just waits for me to reappear. I know we're coming to the end of our game soon—when she will hide, and I won't be able to find her."

Project Unconditional has grown far beyond my initial expectations. I have traveled all over the country and in the process made new friends and learned a great deal about dogs, life, and myself. It has also allowed me the delight of working with my daughter, Kacey, a very talented filmmaker, to develop the complementary video series, *Unconditional Stories.*

Project Unconditional has provided me a deeper appreciation for the commitment people have to their dogs, and how these dogs give back every bit as much—and sometimes more. Spending time with dogs not only brings us great joy, but also teaches us so much about giving and what it means to be human. It is the beauty of the relationships—whether lifelong or newly formed—that inspires me. I hope Project Unconditional inspires you in the same way.

BAILEY

{ 16 YEARS || DACHSHUND || CALIFORNIA }

Dear Diary,

Today is my 16th birthday. I don't know what all the fuss is about. It happens every year. My humans always give me ice cream with dinner and act like it's a big surprise, like I haven't caught on after 16 years. I'm wise beyond my years, but I pretend—I go along with it because, why not? And because I love them. And I love ice cream. I've made a list of some other things I love:

- feasting on dirt
- lounging
- doing my business in the rain (just for the thrill of it!)
- the sound of my own bark
- *Pride and Prejudice* (anything by Jane Austen, really)
- sniffing butts and taking names

I've come a long way since my years as a wee pup, and I must say, 16 looks good on me. I've grown quite regal. But now I'm getting writer's paw, and this fashion model needs her beauty sleep. Until next time.

XOX
Bailey

—Aliya Weiss

AVERY

{ 17.5 YEARS ‖ ENGLISH SPRINGER SPANIEL MIX ‖ OREGON }

Where to start? Avery is half of my heart. She came into my life at college graduation as a gift from my mom, who rescued this runt of a litter of Springer Spaniel mixes from a Kentucky kill shelter. I thought I was so not ready for a dog, but Avery knew different. She has helped me grow up and become a better person. She has been by my side through health issues; lost jobs; moves; and the deaths of my grandparents, dad, aunt, and uncle. I started dating my husband a few weeks before she came into our lives, so she's his everything too.

Avery has been in the Atlantic and Pacific, and still takes walks with our other two fur kids. She doesn't make it as far as she used to anymore and prefers to ride home in the stroller. She's half blind and mostly deaf; she's torn both anterior cruciate ligaments and suffers from pancreatitis, thyroid issues, and chronic urinary tract infections.

The doctors have told us that she seems to be in good spirits, so we get to have her with us a little longer. Every day is a gift with her. When she woofs and wags her tail in her sleep, it still makes me smile, and I know all the effort is worth it.

—Jen DeVere Warner

" When she woofs and wags her tail in her sleep, it still **makes me smile,** and I know all the effort **is worth it.** "

CASPIN

{ 8 YEARS ‖ LABRADOR RETRIEVER-GOLDEN RETRIEVER MIX ‖ CALIFORNIA }

Caspin, a Canine Companions for Independence service dog, has been working alongside me for six years. I have dystonia, a muscle disorder that not only makes movement sometimes difficult, it makes speaking nearly impossible. Since we've been working together, Caspin has learned to understand more than 50 commands and communications in American Sign Language.

Caspin has done the impossible: pulling me home during dystonic attacks, instinctively navigating two years of hospitalizations, and anticipating my needs based on cues as simple as following my eyes when I'm stricken and can't move, even to sign. Through partnership with Georgia Tech's FIDO research team, Caspin can even seek help by tugging a rope sensor on a special vest that activates a speaker, which informs a bystander that his owner needs attention.

Together, we are a remarkable team. He has helped me conquer many big challenges: graduating from Gallaudet University for the deaf with honors, competing in an international alpine monoski competition, and moving 3,000 miles from my family home to pursue a dream career. Caspin is my independence, my dignity, my sense of safety, and my best friend.

Together we are not just succeeding, we are thriving.

—Wallis Brozman

23

SPUR

{ 13 YEARS ‖ ALASKAN HUSKY ‖ ALASKA }

Ever since I adopted my 13-year-old retired Iditarod sled dog, we have been inseparable. Spur is my shadow, following me from room to room at home and sticking to my hip at crowded parties. However, when I slip on her harness and we charge out on a snowy trail, it all changes. Spur lives to pull.

We were two miles into a six-mile ski on the night of winter solstice when I stalled on top of a hill. Spur sensed my apprehension, quickly turned and pulled the leash from my grip, and then bolted back toward the trailhead. Devastated, I watched the red light on her collar disappear into the darkness.

I rushed after her with my skiing partner, Joe. He kept reassuring me that she was safe, but I could only imagine the worst. When we got to the trailhead, there she was, curled up in a tight Husky ball by the back tire of the truck. Together we started our skiing adventure again—this time without hesitation. That night Spur reminded me to always stay positive on our outdoor adventures.

My loyal dog serves as a constant source of inspiration. I have yet to see her tired after our daylong adventures: her pulling me on my bike, skis, or dogsled runners. I hope I'm as tough as Spur when I'm in my golden years.

—Mollie Foster

NEBLINA

{ 14+ YEARS ‖ MIXED BREED ‖ MASSACHUSETTS }

"Puppy." Sometime later in her life with me, she got addressed as such, and it stuck. She gets called "Puppy" as much if not more than her given name, Neblina. The name is Spanish and translates to "mist, clouds, fog," which is her coloring (or was, she has a lot more white now). A young fisherman who lived near where I found her offered the name.

Oh, yeah, I found her (or perhaps she found me) out in the desert on the Pacific coast of Baja California, Mexico, while on a camping trip 14 years ago. She was a pathetic little creature and indeed a puppy, though I did not know it at the time. She was nearly starving and covered with fleas and sores. I almost didn't pick her up. But at the urging of a friend, I did, and only minutes passed before I knew I would never set her down. She was terrified of everything, and considering the circumstances out there in the desert, where there is no control of the dog population and no food to speak of, she would not have had much of a future among the coyotes ... You get the picture!

Neblina is a Mexican mutt, native to the Baja desert. She is sleek and slender, and even at this age she can run like a Greyhound. She is remarkably graceful and goes bounding through tall grass like a gazelle. She's incredibly gentle, so much so that a friend even nicknamed her "Gandhi-Puppy."

When I got her home to central Vermont, she stepped out of my truck into snow that almost buried her, but she didn't skip a beat. She stepped right into my life and has been in my home and my heart for almost 14 years now. She won't let me out of her sight, and she is not pleased when I leave her behind (which is difficult for me as well).

There was a time when I'd go trail riding on my mountain bike every day with her at my side. We both seem to have retired from that, and Neblina spends a good amount of her time on her bed, as befits an elderly pup. Still, she and my partner will get to playing and the two of them will go running around the house like a couple of kids. One of many snapshots: Neblina may have a bit of separation anxiety, which she expresses by getting into the soiled laundry pile and getting out one sock, just one, that she'll then deposit on the floor. It is not chewed up. (Though available, she never chooses a clean sock.) She's done that for years, go figure. I am enchanted by the workings in her little head that I will never quite figure out.

People who hear her story comment that it was so kind of me to rescue her. I suppose so, but that kindness is repaid a hundred times a day.

The vet says her heart is getting weak. I feel obligated to let nature take its course and will not medicate her except for her comfort. I hope and pray that I will not have to choose to bring her life to a close.

I have my doubts about humans, but I know there is a heaven for puppies. Neblina. Neblinita. Puppy.

—Tim Rice

GRACE

{ 15 YEARS ‖ BORDER COLLIE ‖ VERMONT }

My family of two humans and a small farm full of goats, chickens, and a barn cat are all a herding dog like me could possibly want. I know I am in my twilight years, but I've still got work to do! Herding goats and chickens? Piece of cake. I often dream of the chase, as evidenced by how fast my legs go in my sleep. (Apparently I talk in my sleep too.)

In my younger days, I was very intense—watching and herding everything in sight, including my stuffed animal toys. If they didn't move on their own, I threw them up in the air myself. Well, I must admit I still do that.

I love my humans. I love how they love me. I get constant pets and, now that I am older, daily massages. They throw my toys around for me, even in the house, and find it entertaining when I pull the exact toy they requested from the basket. They try to involve me in everything they do, including their human jobs. I used to be more independent, but now I want to spend more time with them. I can't do all of the hikes they still do, so they take me on extra "Grace hikes" and let me sniff and dillydally as much as I want. They tell me I am the best dog ever. Maybe I am.

Love,
Grace

—Annie Rubright and Jean Goldsborough

BARBARELLA

{ 13 YEARS ‖ PIT BULL ‖ VERMONT }

This captures a wonderful moment in our life together. If you had met Barbarella, you would have loved her too.

Our relationship was so tight, I often asked myself if I loved her too much, if I bestowed more than I should upon Barbarella.

I didn't think I could live without her. We were a team. We faced everything together. Side by side, we were strong, intelligent, and beautiful. Now my once-in-a-lifetime dog is gone.

The answer is no, I did not love Barbarella too much. Love is never-ending. Thank you for showing me the way, Boobie.

XOXO

—Jennifer Lalli

> We were **a team.**
> We faced everything together.
> Side by side, we were
> **strong, intelligent,**
> **and beautiful.**

LUCY AND SAVVY

{ 14 YEARS AND 13 YEARS ‖ CAVALIER KING CHARLES SPANIEL AND SPANIEL MIX ‖ CALIFORNIA }

I fostered Savvy when she was just a year old. She was a shy dog, and the shelter had difficulty getting her adopted. She bonded to me immediately and put all her trust in me right away. A single, retired woman quickly adopted her. They did well together, but apparently Savvy never forgot me. When her owner passed away six years later, she left Savvy to me in her will. This inspired me to start Peace of Mind Dog Rescue, which takes in dogs from senior citizens and terminally ill people, and also rescues senior dogs from animal shelters.

Lucy came into our lives as a foster right around the time that Savvy came back to us. Lucy's guardians were in their late 80s and having trouble caring for her. Lucy is a happy-go-lucky, soft, sweet, bubbly dog who loves everyone she meets and is afraid of nothing. She is Savvy's exact opposite. It turns out, Lucy became Savvy's therapy dog. As long as Lucy is with Savvy, she is okay with letting strangers pet her and can go to the groomer or vet without being stressed.

Savvy has come a long way, but she still only has eyes for me.

—Carie Broecker

JOE

{ 11+ YEARS OLD ‖ GERMAN SHEPHERD MIX ‖ CALIFORNIA }

I think I was drawn to be in a relationship with an older animal because I, too, am an older animal, and we share a quieter energy. My relationship with sweet, sweet Joe offers joy and an opportunity to experience the complexity inherent in aging. A stray from the streets of Los Angeles, Joe was initially fearful, sad, and barely walking when I adopted him through the Thulani Program, a rescue organization for senior and hospice German Shepherds. Providing Joe with safety, comfort, nurturance, fun, and peace for these years has been a profound experience. I am awed and nourished by his capacity to trust, adjust to change, and thrive.

—Valerie Auerbach

CHEYENNE

{ 17 YEARS ‖ LABRADOR RETRIEVER–AKITA MIX ‖ NEW YORK }

Whether one calls it serendipity, coincidence, or fate, this is how Cheyenne entered my life.

Slightly more than 17 years ago, I was living in Atlanta, Georgia, with my partner, Bill, and together we were looking for "just the right puppy." For a few months we visited our local humane society weekly without any luck. On Super Bowl Sunday 1997, I stopped by the shelter alone, only to find it overflowing with people adopting cats and dogs. I walked around and, much to my dismay, started feeling like Goldilocks. "Too big." "Too small." But wait … "Just right!" I thought to myself when I spotted two puppies snuggled together.

I looked a bit closer only to notice that they both were wearing red tags, indicating their pending adoption. I was ready to leave and try again the following week, but these puppies were so cute that I had to hold them before leaving. I reached in the cage, lifted one of the pups, and there sleeping underneath her siblings was a third puppy with no tag on her collar. I lifted the yellow-and-white-booted puppy into my arms (and my heart), never wanting to let her go.

Cheyenne was so much more than we ever expected from a canine companion. It took Bill a couple years to feel the bond, but once he did, our "pack" was complete. The middle of this story is filled with years and years' worth of experiences (both good and bad) with which any pet lover can identify.

At 16, Cheyenne was slowing down, having survived two bouts of cancer and simply old age. Bill always said, "She's running on pure love." I believe that to be true. At 17, Cheyenne's health took a dramatic turn for the worse. She was rapidly losing weight and not walking on her own. Soon she stopped eating and drinking. Within a couple days, she passed in Bill's loving arms.

—Todd Collins

FREESIA

{ 11 YEARS ‖ LABRADOR RETRIEVER ‖ VERMONT }

One of the great things about being a K9 handler for the Vermont State Police is that you get to bring your best friend to work with you. For eight years, no matter how bad the day, I always had the little black dog (or "LBD," as the troops referred to her). Part certified Explosive Detection Canine, part unofficial departmental therapy dog, Freesia was certainly one of the most popular troopers on the force. No matter if it was the Vermont State House, a local school, or even the administrative offices at the Vermont Department of Public Safety headquarters, Freesia was known by name to many—even if they didn't remember mine.

Although Freesia was still able to do her job after eight years, the department and I felt she had served her time for the citizens of Vermont. She still comes to the door every morning hoping to get called out to the police cruiser, but we have both come to realize it's time for her to enjoy life as a family dog. She gets a pat on the head, a "Be a good girl," and knows she's staying home.

—Bob Lucas

KRINGLE

{ 18 YEARS ‖ MALTESE ‖ NEW YORK }

Kringle is very special. By far the most intelligent dog I've ever had, he makes his needs and desires understood and can anticipate what I want. Except for my children, he is the love of my life—and my constant companion.

When Kringle was eight years old, we moved from a suburban home to an apartment in Manhattan, an environment he truly loved. The building elevator became a place to socialize with adults, children, and other dogs. Activity on the street stimulated him, and he became the consummate shopper, as stores offered the opportunity for new adventures.

We fortunately live near Madison Square Park, and Kringle became a regular occupant of one of the park's benches. He sat through book talks in fair and stormy weather and attended afternoon and evening musical programs. When I had to use a walker after an accident, people commented about how he watched me continuously as we walked along.

The distance to the park now puts a strain on his heart, so I take him in a shopping cart with a blanket padding the bottom. Many times he stands up in the cart to greet interesting passersby. Although he is a senior, he still retains his playfulness and provides me with the kind of joy, love, and companionship that only a dog can give.

—Syd Levy

BENTLEY

{ 14 YEARS ‖ LABRADOR RETRIEVER ‖ INDIANA }

What does Bentley mean to me? Bentley means independence, confidence, and companionship.

I became blind at 14 and got my first guide dog at 17. Before that, I didn't travel much and hardly went out. However, since getting a guide dog, I now have the confidence to travel alone, and that confidence crosses over to all facets of my life.

I have lived in four states since 2006, and Bentley has been the one constant in all my moves and everything I have done. He is part of my family. If he's not welcome somewhere, then I'm not welcome there.

With a guide dog, it's all about trust. If you don't trust your dog, you don't have a guide. During training with Bentley at Guiding Eyes for the Blind, we were crossing the street and a car came around the corner. It would have hit me, but Bentley pushed me out of the way and the car grazed him on the head. He took a hit for me. Bentley didn't miss a beat or become frightened. He went right back into the road with me, and we safely crossed the street. After that incident, I knew Bentley was the dog for me.

Bentley continued

I have had Bentley for 12 years. When he was young, he used to love to run and take big vertical leaps. He can no longer run or jump like he used to, but these days he runs in his sleep. I know he's dreaming about being young. It puts a smile on my face every time he runs in his sleep, but at the same time, a part of me is sad that Bentley can't be young again.

—Jywanza Maye

"
With a guide dog,
it's all about **trust.**
If you don't
trust your dog,
**you don't have
a guide.**
"

MAGGIE

{ 15 YEARS ‖ BORDER COLLIE MIX ‖ VERMONT }

Although the most gentle soul, Maggie has always been a free spirit, not wanting to be confined. At the Rutland County Humane Society, which rescued her as a six-month-old stray, she would climb the chain-link fence of her kennel and sit on the roof. When she came to live with me, she began to scale the fence in the yard. I made it higher and higher, but Maggie, aka "Little Monkey," could scale even a seven- to eight-foot wire fence. She wouldn't go far, however—just stroll the neighborhood, visit the post office, or sit in her driveway until someone let her in.

Maggie's greatest pleasure in life was, and still is, running in the woods. Now at 15, she continues to love her hikes but is content to share them with her mom at a slightly more leisurely pace. We get out together every chance we can.

—Anne Pace

LILA

{ 14 YEARS ‖ SIBERIAN HUSKY MIX ‖ VERMONT }

Although I never had a dog growing up, I always enjoyed the company of dogs. We had all sorts of other animals in our home, but when my daughter and ex-wife visited the shelter and met a dog there, they decided we *needed* a dog in our home. So home we came with Delilah, who quickly became just Lila to us. She was full of energy, exuberance, and reminders of whatever challenges she had faced in her past.

Lila always had lots of energy. She loved her walks, and she loved even more the outdoor adventures we'd find ourselves on, from running with me on roads or trails to hiking, skiing, or snowshoeing. She'd go anywhere.

Lila always thought she was a part of the family, just like everyone else. She would make herself comfortable on any chair or sofa, leap up and snuggle close to anyone, and for many years would try to make herself quite at home in the middle of the bed. She made her funny noises and sighs when she was settled, happy, and comfortable.

One lesson Lila taught me was to live life in the moment. No matter how long she might have been home alone, safe and snuggled in her doghouse, whenever I arrived, she would race out and leap three feet in the air with a joyful greeting. How could you not welcome that, appreciate that, and be grateful for that? Humans could learn from dogs about how to welcome

home loved ones with focus, joy, and appreciation, rather than viewing their arrival as an interruption or an obligation for what's next.

Lila had a good, long, and healthy life. Yes, it was work, but she brought joy and smiles and laughter into our lives. She was a master of living joyfully in the moment. She showed me that if you focus too much on the past or the future, you can too easily lose sight of what is before you in the here and now: frost in the morning, a luminescent sunset in the evening, the crystal clarity of the stars and the sounds in the darkness of night, and the boundless expression of unconditional love and joy when your special person comes home to you at the end of the day.

—Lee Krohn

MULLY

{ 7 YEARS ‖ LABRADOR RETRIEVER ‖ CALIFORNIA }

A boy and a dog: Wesley and Mully.

Their first meeting was not at a pound or a pet store but in our front yard. In half a minute they became friends, which, eight years prior, was how long it took the doctor to diagnose my son's autism. This meeting was not by chance. It was arranged by Tender Loving Canines Assistance Dogs, and it was not without risk. Some children wouldn't make it out of the house, while some dogs wouldn't go in. Not so for Wesley and Mully. It was sweetness from the start.

A rich relationship based on perfect trust and pleasure in one another's company developed. Sometimes it seemed that my son liked nothing more than to listen to the steady beat of Mully's tail on the hardwood floor. With his assistance dog credentials, Mully could go just about anywhere, and Wesley was eager to do just that. In the beginning, I tagged along (as moms do), with Wesley holding both Mully's leash and my elbow. We walked to the bookstore, to the library, to the sculpture garden at the museum. Until one afternoon, Wesley did not reach for my elbow. He held Mully's leash tight in one hand, as his other arm hung at his side. "Mully, with me!" he called out, catching the last few seconds of a green light to cross the street and leaving me behind to wait for the next one. It was all as it should be.

—Claudia Metcalfe

58

BELLA 🐾

{ 15 YEARS ‖ SPANIEL–CHOW CHOW MIX ‖ NEW JERSEY }

Bella and I have been together for 12 years, ever since I rescued her from a New Orleans shelter the day before she was to be euthanized. Or rather, she rescued me, of course.

Adventuring our way across the country, we've traveled together extensively and lived in seven states. She was with me in the Arctic while I was a teacher in an Inupiaq Eskimo village. She was a therapy dog in my classroom full of preschoolers who had suffered abuse at home. The children could talk to her about things they felt unsafe saying to adults. I understand—she's a good listener.

Bella has been my compass. We've hiked together on the tundra and sea ice, in the high desert of New Mexico, in the rain forests of Seattle, and across the midwestern farmland where I was born. Together we've traversed more mountain ranges than I can keep track of.

Now we live in Caldwell, New Jersey, where our days are quieter and our hiking days are over. Instead, we take very, very slow walks in our neighborhood. I can hardly bear knowing that our adventure together will soon draw to a close.

—Kelsea Habecker

She was a **therapy dog** in my classroom . . . The children could **talk to her** about things they felt **unsafe saying to adults.**

LILY

{ 14 YEARS ‖ DOBERMAN PINSCHER-ROTTWEILER MIX ‖ MASSACHUSETTS }

My family was lucky enough to get the last puppy of an abandoned litter from the local animal shelter. She was described as a dominant Beta female who would not be good for us. My, how first judgments can be so very wrong. Lily has been by my side from junior year in high school to our first child. She is now 14 years old and continues to run, swim, chase her ball, and cuddle as if she were still young.

As she protected me, she now watches over our son, ensuring that every cry is answered and no one puts him in danger. Her devotion is nothing short of incredible, and our family is stronger as a result.

I am extremely privileged to have grown up with such a loyal and forgiving sidekick. Lily has always been there to give us her smile, followed by those endless kisses that erase everything else in the world. She exemplifies all the happiness one can find in adopting a shelter dog. Forever love my Lily-bug.

—Scott Beauchemin

COOKIE

{ 14+ YEARS || TERRIER MIX || CALIFORNIA }

Cookie is blind. The kind of blind that denies all light. She lives by her ears, her nose, and her deep trust that we will always be there for her. And we are. All of us.

She lives with Kathleen, me, and Muchacho (Chacho, for short), a poodle-y kind of guy we found behind a bus stop in Juárez, Mexico. He came to us shut down and filled with fear, and he seemed to have no idea how to be a dog. Cookie came to us broken and abandoned, and she put her trust in him. She had to. He was her only hope.

The more she trusted him to guide her, the more he began to act like a dog. She taught him to play. He watched her accept love and affection from us, and he tried it on for himself. She gave him purpose in life. He gave her eyes and his heart, and we watched them open up to each other. And they loved each other, each maybe for the first time.

Now it was our turn to fall in love, with both of them. When you have a foster dog, you have to hold back on the big falling-down-on-your-knees kind of love that happens between dogs and people. You have to allow your heart to gently love your foster dogs and then let them go, so you can foster others and save more dogs' lives.

JAN
www.MUTTVILLE.org
senior dog rescue
California
2018
RSQZ DGS
...because it's never too late for a new beginning!

That's what we did. We gently loved Cookie. We gave her as much healing as we could but held back. Chacho didn't. He rushed into love, unaware that it could be lost. He fell into every moment with her. She made him feel safe and let him experience the dog joy he had lost in order to survive. He made her feel part of a family and gave her confidence. She had no idea that she should hold back, so she didn't.

We took her to all the Muttville adoption events, but our remarkable, smart, and incredibly resilient blind girl became a monster at each opportunity to be adopted. She barked insanely. She jumped over the exercise pens the adoptable dogs shared. Adopters moved away from her. She would come home with us exhausted from her protests but ready to tumble into play with Chacho. It was obvious she wanted to be with him. And us. After the last adoption event we took Cookie to, we got down on the floor with them and we, too, started to let go and plunge into their tumble together. Head over heels, bellies up, hearts opening, we began to fall in love.

Cookie and Chacho are our family now. Our blind dog is our greatest teacher, and our terrified Mexican rescue is our greatest joy. Together they have given us more than we could ever have hoped for. Love, compassion, tenderness, and huge joy.

—Deirdre Kidder

JACK

{ 10+ YEARS ‖ GOLDEN RETRIEVER ‖ VERMONT }

Jack was our best exercise machine. Some days you just didn't feel like going for a walk, but he'd look at you with those deep, pleading eyes and ... well, how could you resist? Snowshoeing up the mountain was our favorite exercise. Dave and I would plod through the snow, while Jack bounded, covering at least ten times the distance.

No matter how far or how long we hiked, we'd be whipped when we returned home. Meanwhile, wanting to continue to play, Jack would search for a tennis ball to drop at our feet. The hike had only whetted his appetite for more exercise.

(Sidebar: I've wondered, prior to the invention of tennis balls, what did Golden Retrievers retrieve?)

Jack, you were a wonderful friend, and we all miss you very much.

—Jill Sands

CHLOE

{ 9 YEARS ‖ PEKINGESE ‖ MASSACHUSETTS }

You're never too old, too sick, too poor, too anything to find joy. I find it every day with my Chloe.

If it weren't for Chloe, I'd probably spend all day in my apartment watching television. I'd feel sorry for myself. I might even give up on life. But every day when I get up and take Chloe out to the park—me in my wheelchair, Chloe walking along beside me—I feel like the luckiest man in the world. When she gets tired and wants to be picked up, she stops and head-butts my wheelchair.

We understand each other. We have ice cream together. We do everything together.

—Waymon Simmons

> You're **never** too old, too sick, too poor, too anything **to find joy.**

JOSIE

{ 10 YEARS ‖ ENGLISH MASTIFF ‖ MASSACHUSETTS }

Her real name is Josie Lu Blue. When I adopted her, she weighed eight pounds, and I promised my husband she would not be big. Well, I kind of lied—at her peak she was 225 pounds. It's like having a zoo animal in your home. She is the sweetest, calmest friend I have.

Josie has many nicknames—lately I call her "DoRight." Maybe because she can't do wrong. My daughter's friends call her "ShoeDog." Every week while my daughter was in college I sent her a picture of Josie wearing a pair of my shoes. It definitely got a laugh out of stressed-out college girls.

So Josie, DoRight, ShoeDog—whatever name we call her—is just the medicine I need. She has never been very active, nor social with other dogs, nor difficult. She is a ten-year-old girl who loves her family. She is a protector of us all. She just wants to be loved and needed, kind of like her mom.

So I give to her what she gives to me. I'm very lucky to have my Josie.

—Stacy Cohen

STORM AND THUNDER

{ 10 YEARS AND 8 YEARS ‖ MIXED BREEDS ‖ ILLINOIS }

Storm and Thunder are ideal dogs. When we wake in the morning, they'll come to each side of the bed and check that my wife, Julie, and I are both there and okay, with a nuzzle and gentle lick.

They're also very gentle with toys, which they treat more like puppies, licking, grooming, and rarely chewing. They've had the same toys since the day we picked them up from PAWS Chicago—and of course, they've received new ones too!

Storm and Thunder are the kind of dogs that love all people, especially Julie and me. They don't like being apart from one another or from us for any amount of time. They'll invade the bathroom just to have company. If we leave the room for five minutes, we can expect to be greeted with a full welcome upon our return.

—Travis Lee

SCOTTIE, WAWA, SANDRA DEE

{ 12 YEARS, 11 YEARS, 10 YEARS ‖ BICHON FRISE, CHIHUAHUA, MALTESE ‖ ILLINOIS }

We found Pippen, a spunky terrier, on the Greek island of Crete. As with many strays, he would have been poisoned by local farmers after the tourist season ended. We could not leave this adorable pup to such a cruel fate.

My daughter and I were shocked to learn that homeless cats and dogs in Chicago did not fare much better. They were taken to shelters where the majority—more than 40,000 each year—were killed. In response, we founded PAWS Chicago in 1997 as a comprehensive humane organization. The number of pets dying needlessly in Chicago has been reduced by nearly 77 percent since then. Pippen died on October 25, 2005, but his legacy lives on.

Our family continues to honor Pippen's memory by adopting older dogs. We currently share our home with Scottie, Wawa, and our newest addition, Sandra Dee. In November 2014, PAWS stepped in to save nine Maltese dogs who had been brought, covered in filth, to the city pound by a breeder. One of these special dogs was Sandra Dee, whom I fostered and later adopted. She loves to follow me around and stands so close to my feet that sometimes I don't see her. When I look down, she is staring up at me, and all I feel is love.

—Paula Fasseas

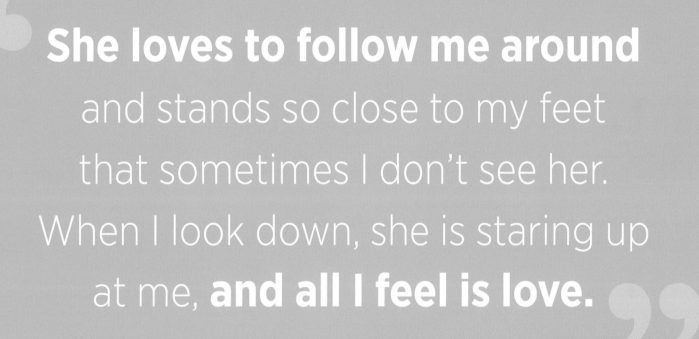

She loves to follow me around and stands so close to my feet that sometimes I don't see her. When I look down, she is staring up at me, **and all I feel is love.**

PATTY

{ 13 YEARS ‖ PIT BULL ‖ CALIFORNIA }

The first time I saw Patty I could have cried. As an animal control officer, I've seen some pretty terrible things. But Patty was so starved and neglected that even I was shocked. She was elderly, with clouded eyes and infected skin. She was even missing teeth. What really touched me was how happy and excited she was when I spoke to her. She melted me on the spot. Her old, hairless tail was wagging so hard that she almost fell over, and I wrapped my arms around her and promised her a better life.

She walked her skinny, bald self into my house and surveyed her kingdom. So powerful was her presence that she sweetly greeted my mature, bossy, female dogs with the equivalent of "Hello, friends. I'm your new queen," and they bowed to her on the spot. They were all bigger than Patty, but she never postured, growled, or lifted a lip. They just accepted her.

It was such a joy to watch Patty grow stronger every day while she took delight in every comfort provided. She has blessed our home a hundredfold. A pit bull ambassador to everyone she meets, she is a comforting presence to all the kittens, puppies, broken dogs, scared dogs, and old dogs that come through our home as fosters. Every night as I tuck her into her thick cushy bed next to mine, I kiss her in the dip between her big brown eyes and feel thankful that she came into our lives.

—Shirley Zindler

HANNA

{ 12 YEARS ‖ GOLDEN RETRIEVER ‖ OREGON }

Why is it that we only pause to remember when someone is ill or has died? Well, I've decided that I am not going to wait until Hanna is gone to celebrate all she has given me.

When Hanna's time comes, I will be an utter mess—a scrape-me-off-the-floor-in-pieces mess. People may think I am silly, but I love her like she is my child, my best friend, and my soul mate. I can't imagine these last 12 years without her by my side.

She came to me as surprise Christmas present from my husband, John. That Christmas he also gave me the gift of climbing mountain peaks with Hanna, swimming in the ocean and streams with her, and having her lick the tears off my cheek when I am sad. Without that gift, I wouldn't know what it's like to let the kids read to her and climb on her back, to stroke her crimped ears, or to watch her carry ten-pound rocks in her mouth for miles on the trail. I would never have watched her put herself to bed in our camping tent or inhaled the sweet scent of earth on her paws after a long day of hiking on Mt. Hood. If I could bottle that smell and keep it with me for the rest of my life, I would. But for now I am going to settle for giving her a great big hug.

—Sheryl Maloney

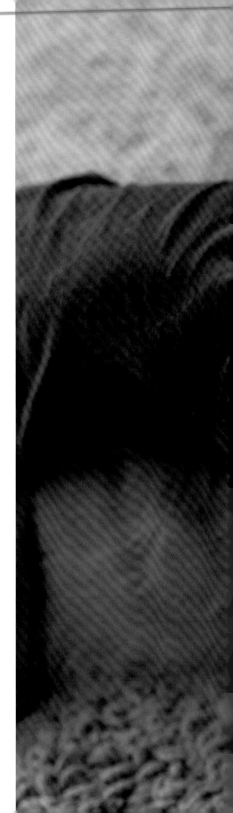

CODY

{ 9 YEARS ‖ AUSTRALIAN CATTLE DOG ‖ TEXAS }

I didn't teach this dog anything. He just knows. As soon as I put him on the truck at eight weeks old, we connected. Cody has a mind of his own. My wife says that he's an alien. His mom was a Blue Heeler, and his daddy was a Red Heeler. His teeth are filed because he herds the cows. When a cow isn't moving, he'll nip the cow on the leg. That is his job.

He's with me 24 hours a day. He sleeps right beside my bed. If I go to the bathroom, Cody's there waiting when I open the door.

Cody knows the order of how I get ready in the morning. If I get dressed first, he knows we aren't going to work, and he stays and relaxes. If I put on my socks first, he knows it's time for work, and he gets up immediately and eats his food.

My wife hates when Cody smiles because she thinks he is laughing at her.

Men will come to the ranch from all over the world to look at our cattle for sale. They will always try to buy Cody because he's so good with the cows.

I tell them, "If I sold you Cody, I'd be ripping you off because he won't do anything for you." I say, "Try to tell Cody to do something."

They try. Cody just walks away.

I wouldn't change anything about Cody.

—Barbarito "Blackie" Heredia

MOLLY

{ 10+ YEARS ‖ MALTESE ‖ CONNECTICUT }

Molly is my gift from heaven. She came into my life on the first anniversary of my beloved husband, Don's, death. We are now inseparable. She looks at me with such adoration, as if to tell me how grateful she is to be mine. She knows how thankful I am to have her help fill such a tremendous loss.

Molly was rescued from a breeder in Missouri, who had surrendered her when her "services" were no longer needed. She was nine when we found each other, and I wish she could tell me everything that happened to her before we met. She knows well all that happened to me.

Now I am weepy, so I will close.

—Shirley Calcaterra

COCO, EDITH, ROXY, STELLA

{ 10 YEARS, 12 YEARS, 11 YEARS, 11 YEARS ‖ CHIHUAHUA MIX, POMERANIAN MIX, CHIHUAHUA MIX, FRENCH BULLDOG ‖ CALIFORNIA }

Senior dogs became a passion of ours after Rafael and I were introduced to Sherri Franklin, the founder of Muttville Senior Dog Rescue. We were immediately inspired and wanted to contribute, so we offered to foster a dog. I remember her placing in my arms a little dog named Misty Kay Mabelline. She was certainly odd looking, with big eyes, a tongue hanging out of her mouth, and back legs longer than the front, making her look like she was walking on high heels. She was a cranky old lady of a dog, but after having her for a couple of weeks, we fell in love. Misty Kay became a permanent member of our home until she passed away three years later.

We continue to foster other senior dogs in need and have taken in as many as 30 over the years. Many of these dogs enter our house traumatized from losing their homes. Others come with medical issues that need to be treated.

Saying goodbye to our foster dogs is always bittersweet. But although we miss every single one of them, the need is too great not to continue. So, with a heavy heart, we say goodbye, wipe away the tears, then say hello to the next frightened dog that just needs some love.

—Joe Marko

Saying goodbye to our foster dogs is always bittersweet. But although we **miss every single one of them,** the **need is too great** not to continue.

FORREST

{ 13 YEARS ‖ GERMAN SHORTHAIRED POINTER ‖ CALIFORNIA }

I adopted Forrest from a rescue when he was about 18 months old, and he has been my constant companion for almost 12 years. For a short time, he was an only dog, after one of my other German Shorthaired Pointers passed away. I could tell he missed the companionship, so we adopted Jenny, a sweet and crazy three-year-old. The size of our family later grew, when Teri, Kelsey, and Hope became part of the pack. Kelsey and Forrest became each other's shadows. When we lost Kelsey, Forrest mourned along with the rest of us, and shortly afterward, his health began to decline.

Forrest's symptoms pointed to degenerative myelopathy, an incurable disease of the spine. He began to lose strength in his hind legs and needed help to get around. But he showed no sign of giving up; his boisterous spirit refused to quit. So we decided we'd do whatever we could to help him.

We researched wheelchairs and selected one we thought best. He took to it right away, almost as if he knew it was there to help him, and began acting like a dog half his age, running around the park chasing after his sisters. When the disease began to affect his front legs, we added front wheels to the wheelchair. Still, nothing has dampened his spirit.

Forrest is still wild and crazy, and now he has a cool set of wheels too!

—John Hembree

PRECIOUS

{ 12 YEARS ‖ COCKER SPANIEL ‖ NEW JERSEY }

I'd always wanted a Cocker Spaniel, but as with most things, timing is everything. At 25, I was nearing the end of a four-year relationship and starting over in a new state. It was the perfect time for me to find a faithful companion that wasn't afraid of a long-term commitment.

I found Precious through a breeder online, and 12 weeks later, I locked eyes with my "precious" cargo at the airport. She quickly became my trusty sidekick. One night my best friend and I were planning to go to a party in Washington, D.C., when we received a call that it was canceled. We weren't about to waste the night, so we decided to drive to another party—in Brooklyn, New York!

We arrived with six-month-old Precious, whom I'd brought along in her small crate. I left my girlfriend to walk her, and when I came back a few minutes later, she was standing on the sidewalk with an empty crate. Frantic, I asked her where Precious was, and she said, "I don't know! Some guy asked me what was in the crate, and he opened it and took her out and ran down the street."

I caught a glimpse of a stranger with my puppy, and after a few minutes, a shadowy figure came running down the street, laughing, with Precious in tow. I shot him a dirty look, grabbed my pup, and pushed my way into the party. As the party drew to a close, my girlfriend and I were chatting with the dognapper and his friend. I later called my mom and told her I'd met my husband.

We have been married almost five years to the day of that crazy evening. I always say I have Precious to thank for delivering my future to me. I often think about our first few months together, and how I thought it would be just the two of us. But God had a different plan in store. Precious gave me the most precious gifts of all: unconditional love, friendship, faith, and most of all, family. I am forever indebted to her.

How's that for a "long-term commitment"?

—Tichanda Thompson

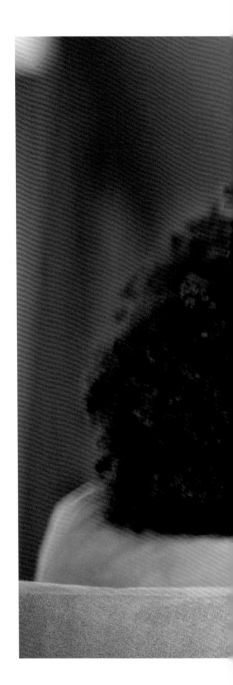

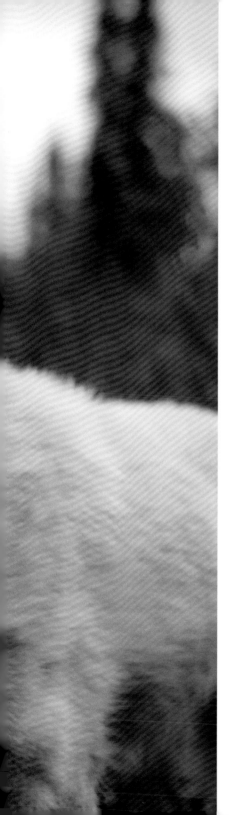

SPOT AND LIGHTNING 🐾

{ 15 YEARS AND 14 YEARS ‖ ALASKAN HUSKIES ‖ ALASKA }

Spot and Lightning are two "golden oldies" of our Salty Dog Kennel, named for our first retired Iditarod sled dog, Salt. In his prime, Lightning was the lead dog, ever eager to run ahead of the others. He guided the team over mountain passes, across rivers, and down hundreds of miles of wilderness trails. Earnest, steady, and gentle, Lightning mentored many of our kennel's young leaders who learned by running at his side.

While Lightning was busy up front, Spot's specialty was to run wheel, the position just in front of the dog sled. Agile, athletic, and spunky, he was quick to help steer the sled around trees, open water, or holes in the trail. Always a hunter, Spot still loves to sniff the tracks of a nearby fox or pounce on an unsuspecting red-backed vole that scampers in front of the team.

Lightning and Spot have long been buddies. While they are now retired and no longer run with the team, they live for salmon treats and ambles through summer's lush tundra or along snow-laden trails. With aging voices, these two often lead our dog team's midnight serenades. Spot, the soprano, sounds the first note; Lightning, the baritone, responds. Then follows a sweet melodic howl, 27 dogs strong: a primordial harmony linking their lives and mine.

—Debbie Clarke Moderow

PIPPEN

{ 12 YEARS ‖ DOBERMAN PINSCHER–BEAGLE MIX ‖ MAINE }

Our relationship is one of the woods. We are both most comfortable there, relishing the beauty and the solitude that it offers.

When confined to the house, Pippen is aloof, slightly nervous, and guarded. Release her to the woods, and she's a different dog. While the sounds and motions within the house create tension and unease in her, those of the forest intrigue her and appeal to her nature. Her tail comes up, her ears go forward, and her aura becomes one of contentment.

Pippen and I have etched our relationship in the hours spent exploring. We sometimes wander off the beaten path, getting just a little lost, following overgrown stone walls, small streams, and subtle paths traced by traveling deer.

Other days we are content to simply follow the well-worn trail. We relax into the meditative rhythm that comes from repetitive motion, without the need for organized thought. Mile after mile passes under our feet. When it's time to head back, I only have to turn my body and Pippen takes the lead in the opposite direction. I follow her with complete confidence that she will lead us safely home.

It's **a look** to make sure I'm there, **to let me know** that although she is not right by my side, **we are on this journey together.**

Always ahead, but never too far, Pippen moves with an athletic, highly efficient trot. With no unnecessary movement, she smoothly glides forward. She used to travel for hours like that, with no sign of fatigue, but over the years she's slowed a bit. We both have.

I will always retain the image of Pippen trotting ahead of me on the long trail, stopping just long enough to look back. It's a look to make sure I'm there, to let me know that although she is not right by my side, we are on this journey together.

—Amy Brown

SHELBY

{ 10+ YEARS ‖ PEMBROKE WELSH CORGI ‖ VERMONT }

Oh, you Corgis. I first saw you little guys in a book on dog breeds, and it was love at first sight. Perhaps it was your structure or the big ears—or maybe your funny-looking butts. It didn't matter. I was enchanted.

Thirty years have passed, and God has blessed Debbie and me with seven of these amazing companions. Calling them companions is like calling a Ferrari a mode of transportation; however, I am at a loss for a better word. They have helped us endure tough times and celebrated with us in good times. All the while filling our lives with the unfailing love and mirth they are so capable of.

Shelby came into our lives like a tempest and took on the demeanor of a precocious kid—an ugly ducking, you might say. When my beloved Tegan, shop dog and constant companion for 15 years, went back to God, Shelby started to fill her paw prints bit by bit, emerging as a beautiful swan. She is still demanding, though. Food and rides in the truck are her top priorities, with Debbie and I being third on the list. Always watching her human charges from a polite distance, Shelby gives love and affection as needed—but always on her terms. Such is a Corgi.

Shelby, Tegan, Pebbles, Suzie, Brindle, Prince, and Curry, we love you so.

—Robert Gutbier

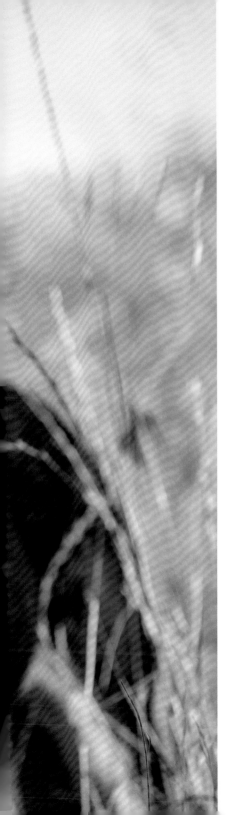

MISSY

{ 10 YEARS ‖ AUSTRALIAN KELPIE-BORDER COLLIE MIX ‖ CALIFORNIA }

Missy came to Lily's Legacy Senior Dog Sanctuary a few months after her owner passed away. At age nine, Missy had lost the only person she knew as Mom. A short stay with relatives had been disastrous, as she was attacked by the resident dogs. She arrived at Lily's Legacy hoping for a new, safe, and loving home. That's where I found her.

She had been through a lot and picked up some bad habits between her owner's passing and when she was surrendered to the sanctuary, where I am a longtime volunteer. In order to help her get adopted, I decided to foster Missy and give her a course in "doggie charm school." Well, she charmed her way directly into our hearts and never left. When she came to my home, my existing pack of two dogs and two cats gave her the once-over and decided she could stay. By the time all the dogs and cats were eating together harmoniously, my husband said, "She's not going back!"

Missy is the first one down the stairs to greet us when we return home. And she's the first one up the stairs when it's time for bed. She has made herself at home on the sofa, on the bed, and in our hearts. I am at peace knowing that when her time comes to cross the Rainbow Bridge, her other mom will be there to greet her and will know just how much Missy was loved.

—Linda Mannella

BIJOU 🐾

{ 13 YEARS ‖ STANDARD POODLE ‖ VERMONT }

Bijou made the transition from a fancy-cat city Poodle to a woodchuck-warrior country Poodle after my husband and I met walking our pups in a dog park in Minneapolis. We promptly forged a new life together and decided to move somewhere we could have a relationship with the land—and provide lots of room for Bijou and his best bud, Caleb, to romp.

The boys became presiding princes over our 30-acre parcel in Vermont named True Love Farm. They've protected vegetable, blueberry, and flower crops with limited success but with great joy and style. In his friskier days, Bij would alert us to a deer in the kale and has always particularly enjoyed a good snuggle in the late-afternoon sun.

—Karen Trubitt

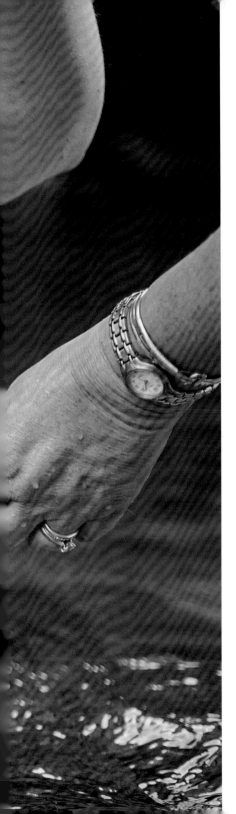

OZZIE

{ 13+ YEARS ‖ AUSTRALIAN KELPIE-SHEPHERD MIX ‖ VERMONT }

My dear Ozzie was held at the shelter for six months, the staff nurturing him and exerting caution about adopting him to just anyone—they feared that his strong looks and size would find him used as a "junkyard dog." One day a friend encouraged me to take a peek at the shelter dogs. How could I resist? Ozzie and I met in the playroom and instantly hit it off. I knew he was a large, strong-willed dog, so I spent the next month visiting the shelter a few times a week to make sure he would be a good fit.

When he came home with me, he quickly made me aware that herding dogs need to roam—for miles! Thus began the journey with one of the strongest and smartest dogs I've ever encountered. Ozzie's spirit to roam but always come home resonates with my own. No fence can keep him in. We don't want to bother anyone, but the urge to discover new territory is unstoppable.

At the time I was single, and Ozzie offered protection, but he was also welcoming and gentle with people of all ages. With his cat friend, Gracie Sage, by his side, the two of them made sure the world was right.

Ozzie and I may be free souls, but we always return home to where our hearts are. Never have I had a dog who understands me as well as he does. Never has he wavered in being there for my family and me.

—Seline Skoug

121

SAMPSON

{ 14 YEARS ‖ CHIHUAHUA ‖ COLORADO }

When life has literally brought me to my knees from pain or sadness, my best buddy, Sampson, is there to lick away the tears and give me nose nibbles and love. When I'm depressed, he always insists on a walk in the morning or tries to trick me into thinking, "Timmy's in the well again." A small something that will get me up and moving.

He loves his blinged-out collar and riding in my Cadillac. Everyone knows him and has special treats for him. Christmas cards are always addressed to Sampson—spelled with a *p* or he's offended—and Albert.

Oblivious to his size, he guards our house and me. He loves me and counts on me, and I hope I am equally there for him. He has turned out to be my perfect life partner. I think I will go kiss him and give him a chicken treat right now and say, "Thank you, best friend."

—Albert Feeger

122

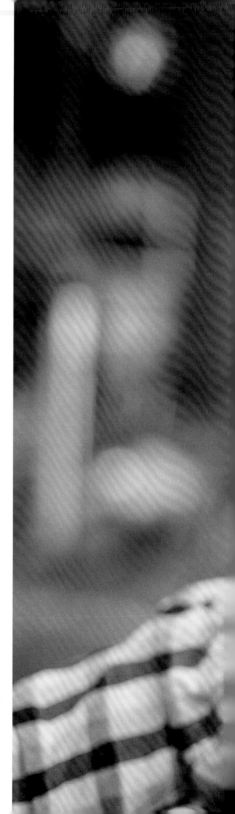

" Oblivious to his size, he guards our house and me. **He loves me** and counts on me, and **I hope I am equally there for him.** "

SAVANNAH

{ 12 YEARS ‖ NEWFOUNDLAND ‖ ARIZONA }

Life is full of connections—friends and family, lovers and acquaintances. We give a little to some and a little more to others. But the connection with a dog who will love you with all their heart, no matter your appearance, mood, or health, is the kind of thing we should strive to share with people too.

I was at the shelter feeling sad, stunned, and confused after a rough loss. As I sat with my back against her kennel, Savannah came up and shoved me with her paw to get my attention, as Newfoundlands do. It took her a couple tries, but when I finally turned around, I saw a sad puppy. Yet she had looked beyond the frightening and uncomfortable confines of her cage to nudge the sad man at her kennel door. We've been together ever since.

—Sam Gutierrez

LULU

Lulu came into my life when I decided to find a wife for my beloved male Pug, Buddha. They were hence married, and a litter followed in quick succession. Knowing that there would be more litters to come, I found great homes for the pups.

Sure enough, their deep love for each other produced another litter of four girls. Sadly, Pugs' infant survival rate is low because their flat noses can cause them to inhale their mother's milk, which leads to pneumonia. Two puppies died, and a third was near death until a phenomenal vet saved her. She is now a beautiful five-year-old.

I was about to find homes for the girls when Buddha died from an overdose of anesthesia during an MRI to determine why his back legs were beginning to wobble. He was only seven years old. Lulu's grief was so intense that within two weeks of his death, her black mask turned pure white. To this day, if I mention his name, she jumps up and looks around eagerly, then lies down with the saddest look on her little white face.

But otherwise, Lulu is an extremely active, happy, deeply devoted old girl. She is devoted to me and to her daughters, who she still regularly cleans, cuddles, plays with, and lovingly disciplines as if they were still puppies. She affectionately watches as they steal food from her bowl.

Although they each have their own doggie bed, they all nap together in Lulu's small bed and spoon each other, with Lulu's front leg draped around their shoulders.

Lulu is my dear little angel. Although she is older now, her spirit is as young as on that wonderful day when I first saw her, and I am confident that she will continue to give us joy, love, and devotion long after she heads off to the Rainbow Bridge.

—Astrid Gifford

JAKE

{ 10+ YEARS ‖ GORDON SETTER ‖ NEW YORK }

Hikers found Jake in the wilderness south of Portland, Oregon. He was skin and bones and clearly had had an abusive past.

I had wanted a dog of my own since childhood, and I recalled the beauty and affectionate personalities of my aunt's Gordon Setters. While daydreaming on Petfinder.com, I found only one match. It was a dog with the sweetest black face, cute brown eyebrows, and a patch of white fur around his throat that my friend refers to as his "ascot tie."

When Jake jumped out of the van at our first meeting, his tail was so tightly tucked between his legs I thought it was docked. I had never met a dog with so much fear. His foster family eventually put his favorite blanket in my car and coaxed him in. That's when I first got to pet his sweet, soft head. When I stopped petting him for a second, I felt a nudge from his nose on my hand. How could I deny this fearful creature something he desired? He stole my heart then and there.

I cannot undo all the damage done in his past, but one thing is certain: He has a club, and if you are in that club, you will be blessed with his affection. You are my rock, Mr. Woof Head! Thank you for trusting me and letting me into your inner circle.

—Emilie McKittrick

MAX

{ 12+ YEARS ‖ LABRADOR RETRIEVER ‖ FLORIDA }

Some gifts come in large boxes clad in red wrapping paper, with bows and ribbons flowing. Others arrive not all at once but over time—and change how you look at the world and alter for the better what kind of person you become. Max was both of these gifts.

Max did not arrive on Christmas morning. He came four weeks later, amid the backdrop of a snowy New Jersey winter. The ground was covered with three feet of freshly fallen snow, and Max, a seven-week-old yellow Lab, bounded and virtually disappeared into the white powdery soft clouds. Worn out from his first adventure in the snow, we wrapped him, sleeping soundly, in a large, red box just before our youngest son, Michael, returned home from school. Over the years, whenever we looked at Max, we remembered the absolute joy and wonder on Michael's face the day he peered into that box to see him for the first time, as well as our oldest son Brian's astonishment when he met his four-legged brother.

Max always approached life with enthusiasm, love, and affection for everyone. Of course everyone says that about their dog, but Max possessed a unique, intuitive ability to sense what we would be doing almost before we did. He seemed to know when we were leaving the house before we indicated it and stationed himself strategically in anticipation. Max didn't simply wag his tail, he wagged his entire body, from the tip of his snout to the very tip of his tail. He was the only dog we've ever seen who had a smile on his face for everyone he met.

A young pup has boundless energy and an eager enthusiasm for learning new things as he matures. But of all the attributes a dog can possess, it is the unrestrained love that remains most important. Each day with Max was a gift.

—Deborah and Bob Cargo

> "Max didn't simply wag his tail, he **wagged his entire body,** from the tip of **his snout** to the very tip of **his tail.**"

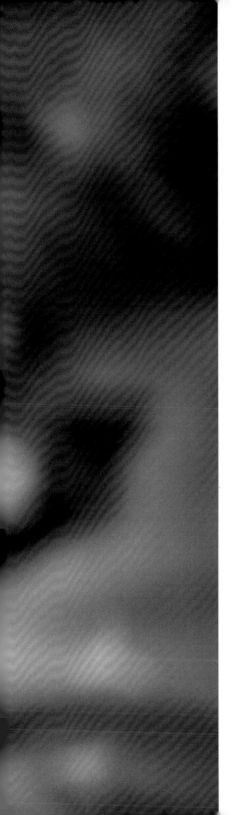

CLEMENTINE

{ 9 YEARS || ENGLISH BULLDOG || VERMONT }

Clementine has a wonderful, quirky personality that has always made me certain that she communicates with me. The tilt of her head, the look in her eyes, her enthusiasm when I come home, and her joy when we play with her toys have been the greatest evidence that her love for us is real and unconditional. And we have unconditional love for her in return.

One year for my wife Angela's birthday, we (and of course, Clemmie) went to Le Château Frontenac in Quebec for the weekend. We told the front desk we were celebrating a birthday, thinking maybe they would bring us strawberries and chocolate! About an hour after we checked in, there was a knock on the door, and sure enough, there was the hotel manager with a big package. We thought it must be for Angela's birthday, until he said, "This is for Mademoiselle Clementine. We want to welcome her to our hotel and make sure she is a pampered pooch during her stay." The package contained a basket of treats and toys! We've laughed about that for years. Clementine was definitely a pampered pooch and deserved it all.

She has truly been "our little girl." As Angela and I go through life, we will surely have other dogs we will love, but Clemmie will always have a special place in our hearts and can never be replaced.

—Phil Arbolino

MISS GOOCH

{ 15 YEARS ‖ DACHSHUND ‖ NEW YORK }

To quote the poet Elizabeth Barrett Browning, "How do I love thee? Let me count the ways."

There came a time in my life when my heart was filled with grief, as I had lost all of the family members who were near and dear to me. Then, as miracles do, this munchkin, who was also the last of her line, suddenly came into my life. Her tail was like a metronome, and her eyes were incredible, deep, deep, soulful pools that refused to allow me away from her gaze. She pried open my heart with her gentle paws and her relentless spirit. Voilà!

Miss Gooch's pure love helped to heal my heart, restore my spirit, and change my life. I know she has fewer years before her than behind her, but I also believe—no, I know—her spirit will be with me always.

I love you, Gooch, today and every day. Best friends forever.

—Susan Lee Grant

RUBY

After my wife, Jayne, and I lost our beloved Sparky, we knew we wanted another Golden Retriever. When we felt ready, our friends Don and Barb Ljungblad helped us find a puppy in their home state of Wyoming. Born in July 2001, Ruby was ready to travel with Barb from Wyoming to Alaska the first week of September 2001. I was working as a long-haul pilot at the time, and Ruby came to us days before the September 11 attack. I will always remember what a comfort she was to me as I continued flying during such a tragic time.

Ruby has logged more flight time than some licensed pilots I know. She loves to ride in the airplane, particularly a floatplane, because she knows she gets to go swimming. Another favorite adventure is fishing. Ruby is sometimes in the boat before I have the motor ready! Besides being able to spend time with us, I think she's excited by the alluring smells of the Alaskan wilderness.

Ruby is now 13 years old, but she still has a strong bark, a sprightly gait, and a wagging tail. She can't quite keep up on the long walks she used to love taking with Jayne, but she still gets to tour the neighborhood in the sidecar of my motorcycle.

This beautiful creature has been a wonderful companion to us for many years, and we feel privileged to continue to care for her.

—Mike Koskovich

WALT

{ 10 YEARS ‖ GREAT DANE ‖ TEXAS }

Walton was the name chosen for my new baby, a Great Dane pup, brought to me by my son and his family as a Mother's Day and birthday present. His name was quickly shortened to Walt, and it seemed to fit him perfectly.

Life with Walt is so amazing because of his size and his gentleness. He is full of love, especially for the family and his best friend, Philly, a Chihuahua mix. The times they spend wrestling and playing have given me hours of entertainment. Our early morning walks on the ranch are of the utmost importance to Walt, and this routine has really helped strengthen his legs and keep both of us fit.

Walt is the first dog I have had of my very own. He is mine, totally mine. He loves the company of other people but scans the room to ensure my presence.

His love is so real—so uncomplicated. I am blessed to know this marvelous animal. Walt brings joy to my life, and to a lot of others who snicker when they see this little, gray-haired lady driving around town with his huge head hanging out the rear window.

My boy, Walt.

—Judy Coates

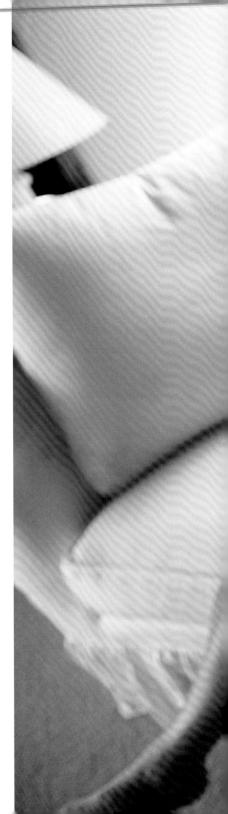

He is mine, **totally mine.**
He **loves** the company
of other people
but scans the room
to ensure my presence.

EINSTEIN

{ 10+ YEARS ‖ SOFT COATED WHEATEN TERRIER MIX ‖ CALIFORNIA }

Einstein arrived at Muttville Senior Dog Rescue on a day I volunteer. He was skinny, matted, and missing hair. His spirit seemed broken, but the boy had a lot of heart. In all honesty, I didn't feel a connection with him right away as I had with some other dogs. He was a little bit of a problem child, so I started hanging out with him. I would take him places such as Golden Gate Park, Bernal Heights, and Ocean Beach, where he saw the ocean for the first time. Then I started to bring him home to hang out, which turned into over-night visits, and my husband and I eventually became his foster parents. In the back of our minds, we knew he kind of picked us.

Einstein is an amazing boy. He loves camping and loves the water. Once he figured out how to swim, he was like a Lab, chasing sticks out in the middle of the lake. He loves sitting in the sun. He eats so many vegetables, we call him a "vege-terrier." Cream cheese is his favorite dessert. He is naturally happy all the time and wags so much that I think his tail got bigger! I can honestly say he's never done anything bad.

He has come such a long way, and we are so proud of him. The reality of it, though, is that my husband and I are really the lucky ones. I couldn't imagine my life without him. He has turned into one of the true loves of my life.

—Miwa Wang

OL' RED

{ 15+ YEARS || BOXER-PIT BULL MIX || CALIFORNIA }

Ol' Red was 15 when he came to Lionel's Legacy, a rescue group with a commitment to saving senior dogs that I founded in 2011. He had recently been diagnosed with lymphoma and was deemed a hospice rescue.

Ol' Red has shown us the true spirit of unconditional love and forgiveness. He has lived a long, rough life, likely from a home where dogs weren't treated as members of the family. When he came to us as a foster, he knew he was in a safe place, and naturally we grew as a family. Our children learned invaluable life lessons from Ol' Red such as patience, empathy, tolerance, and compassion.

Ol' Red helped us see the world through his eyes, to appreciate the sweet simple things in life, and to enjoy each other's company instead of moving at the speed the rest of the world demands. When it comes to rescue groups, everything is about making decisions and coordinating the rescue as soon as it's needed, which unfortunately is often yesterday. At the end of the day, whether we've been able to help or not, Ol' Red is there for us and serves as a reminder of the great work we can do together to advocate for senior dogs in need.

—Laura Oliver

DANNY BOY AND GRACIE 🐾

{ 12 YEARS AND 14+ YEARS || MIXED BREEDS || CALIFORNIA }

When I brought Gracie home from Muttville as my foster dog one rainy night, I had no idea the vital role this terrified little sausage dog would play in my life. In her 12 years, she had never known a kind hand. She deserved to feel safe and loved, and after six months, she grew to trust me. We were still trying to find her a forever home, but Gracie decided she was already home. And without a single adoption application to her name, it seemed the universe was conspiring to keep us together too. And it worked.

Now Gracie is my touchstone, the calming force that holds down one corner of the couch while the hectic world spins around her. The quality of the time we have together far outweighs any concerns about quantity—in fact, having a senior dog reminds me to do something special and joyful every day. Just in case.

Which leads me to Danny Boy. His mission is to help people realize that today is awesome. Like me, he loves to be outside exploring hiking trails at a senior dog's mellow pace.

Danny had been loved his whole life, but when his owner died, there was no plan for him. Muttville stepped in and rescued him from a shelter.

After he came to foster with us, we discovered his cancer and enrolled him in Muttville's hospice program. Danny has lust for life, and after caring for many other dogs with cancer, we knew better than to bring him down with chemotherapy. With supportive care and, most important, a daily dose of happiness, Danny is now doing well. He wants people and their dogs to know that having a limited amount of time isn't tragic—unless you waste it being sad!

—Russell Ulrey

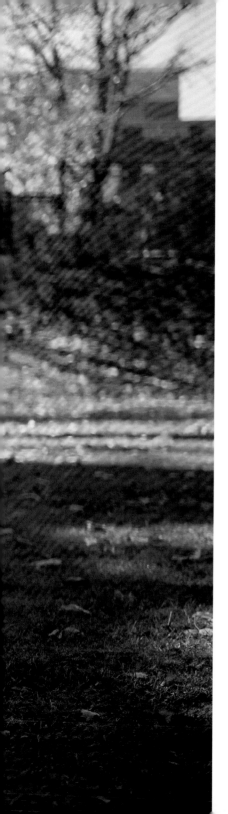

ELVIS

{ 8 YEARS ‖ LABRADOR RETRIEVER ‖ CONNECTICUT }

Imagine spending 24/7 with someone. Never going away on vacation without them, never staying at someone else's house without them. You are *never* apart. Now imagine that person is tied to your body for a good portion of each day, and they know your every movement by heart. They follow the direction of your fingers when you point. They follow your eyes when you stare. They hang on your every word, even when you're not addressing them, just waiting for the opportunity to assist you in some small way. Imagine there's someone whose entire life and happiness depends on your happiness and safety. I can't imagine anything more stressful and selfless all at once.

So I am sitting here looking at my white-faced best friend, confidant, caretaker, protector, and extension of my own body, wondering, "When, buddy? When will it be your time? In six months? Will we have years? Will you tell me when you're ready to retire? How will I be able to let go of that harness handle for the last time? Will you be happy hanging with my mom all day in your retirement? Will it be 'enough' for you?"

I shake my head and get choked up when I realize that, had I chosen to use a cane these past five years, and had I not received the greatest gift that is Elvis from Guiding Eyes for the Blind, how sad and lonely a blind person I think I would be. I know for sure that I wouldn't have had the strength to endure 15 painful eye surgeries in four years without him at every single procedure and office visit, lying quietly next to the exam chair. Each time I got the terrible news that my blindness was progressing and that we needed to go back to the operating room, I could reach down to my right side to scratch his head nervously and be instantly soothed by a heartfelt Labrador gently licking my hand. I would not be the confident, capable, and brave woman that I am today had I not made by far the best decision I've made since my diagnosis.

So here's to Elvis and to hopefully another three good years together—or as long as he tolerates my shenanigans. I think my dancing on bars, waving a sword, and competing in triathlons has prematurely aged this poor, dedicated, four-legged soul. God bless my tall, handsome, blond guy. And I thank God for each and every day he has been part of my life, making me whole again when I was so, so broken.

—Amy Dixon

Imagine there's someone whose **entire life** and happiness **depends on your happiness** and **safety.**

BUDDY

{ 10 YEARS ‖ BEAGLE ‖ COLORADO }

I can thank my granddaughter's Beagle, Vinny, for showing me the light. Until I met Vinny, I never had much interest in dogs, nor did I understand why people became so attached to them. It wasn't long after meeting Vinny that I found my beloved Buddy at the Humane Society of Boulder Valley. We've been inseparable companions ever since.

Buddy has always been a sweet dog, but during his younger years, he occasionally ran off into the hills in search of foxes, chewed up a favorite shoe or shirt, and got a bit hysterical on summer nights when raccoons were prowling the deck or raiding the grape arbor. Now, after nearly ten years of sensing and adapting to the rhythms, habits, and lifestyle of his human and feline family, Buddy seems to have mellowed nearly to perfection.

—Evans Shaw

MAGGIE AND DAISY

{ 10+ YEARS AND 10+ YEARS ‖ COCKER SPANIEL MIX AND POODLE MIX ‖ CALIFORNIA }

Maggie and Daisy were rescued through Lionel's Legacy Senior Dog Rescue. We both believe that senior dogs are the best kind of dog to adopt because they are ready to be present with the family. This dovetails with our goals for raising our children. On our daily family walks, we teach our children that it is important to be happy and to leave the world a better place by being kind and gentle to the people and creatures around us.

—Katie and Jeremy Hirst

167

DUKAVIK

{ 12 YEARS ‖ CHINOOK ‖ VERMONT }

Hey Dukavik, let's take a walk down memory lane.

Do you remember when we first met? You were with all your brothers and sisters. I saw you and it was love at first sight. I came back the next week, and we went home to Maine together.

Do you remember when we would get in the car and drive across the river to play in the sandpits? There were great big cliffs of sand, and you learned to bodysurf down them. You looked so cute sliding on your belly with your legs outstretched.

Remember when we lived at a Residence Inn for seven months, while I worked at our corporate office? You spent days in the back of the truck with a bale of straw for warmth; I would walk you all over the complex at lunch. What a time—at least we were always together.

Now that we are both older, we do quieter things together. You are always at my feet, no matter where I am.

I saw **you** and it was **love at first sight.**

I know that you love your red sweater because, when I wash it, you always look for it in the laundry. I love seeing you in it—it's really your color.

We have been friends for a long time, and I will love you long after you leave. I will find you at the Rainbow Bridge, where we can go running over the fields together again.

I love you, Bud.

—Patti Richards

TREVOR

{ 10 YEARS ‖ CORGI-COCKER SPANIEL MIX ‖ CALIFORNIA }

I adopted my first dog, Trevor, from Muttville Senior Dog Rescue. Our first day together was April Fools' Day 2014. I fell in love with his eyes when I saw his photo; he looked so anxious and vulnerable. Muttville tried to warn me against taking him on, as he is what we euphemistically call a "fear biter." But I was in love.

Trevor has adorable Corgi paws that face sideways and silky, floppy, Cocker Spaniel ears. He doesn't have fur so much as he has fluff. He's got huge soulful eyes that seem to never blink, and he just stares. He looks like a panda bear. He's my stubborn, bad-to-the-bone, fluffy beast. I adore him.

Trevor just wants a quiet, sleepy life on the couch, with his naps interrupted only for ear rubs and chicken. We do things at his pace, and in return, I get to have a furry companion by my side to adore and spoil and ensure that his last years are the very best they can be.

—Colette Dunleavy

AUDREY

{ 11 YEARS ‖ CHIHUAHUA-DACHSHUND MIX ‖ CALIFORNIA }

I never had a dog growing up, although I pleaded with my parents, as most children do, that I simply couldn't live without one. When I got older, I finally took the plunge, and Audrey, a senior Chiweenie (Chihuahua-Dachshund mix), came into my life.

She was abandoned, found as a stray, and ended up at a shelter, where a rescue group saved her and two other senior dogs moments before their termination. She was with the rescue group for six months because no one thought there was anything special about her. I am so fortunate that they were wrong.

Audrey entered my life and that was it. I think we both knew we were meant for each other. In our first moments together, I laid down a blanket and just sat near her. She leaped over me, wagged her tail furiously, and continued to prance around me. It took a long time before Audrey's true personality emerged, but after several years, her confidence, intelligence, opinion, and vocabulary are in full force.

The day I adopted Audrey, I made a promise that we would be together for the rest of her life. She promised to love and protect me through her gentle nose-butt and "that look" that requires no words. I am grateful that she entered my life. Our best years together are yet to come.

—Evelyn Wang

LACI

{ 11 YEARS ‖ LABRADOR RETRIEVER ‖ CALIFORNIA }

Laci was selected to be my service dog by the group Tender Loving Canines Assistance Dogs. She has added years to my life. She got me outdoors on walks around the neighborhood. Because of Laci, she and I now know everybody in the neighborhood. I live in the cloistered Carmelite Monastery of San Diego, so we don't usually go out unless we have a reason. Walking the dog became the reason. She has helped us make friends all over the place and has turned into "the queen of Hawley Boulevard."

People just love her. They know her better than they know me. They say, "Where's Laci?" She's simply been a joy.

The whole community of nuns loves her. She's made a difference in every-one's lives here. There's something about the connection between a dog and a person. Recently I read a beautiful quote, "Dogs are the guardians of being." Isn't that lovely? I think there's a lot of truth in that. There's a very unique connection among all the living creatures in the world, but especially between humans and dogs.

—Sister Electa

MALACHI

{ 10 YEARS ‖ SHIH TZU ‖ NEW YORK }

In 2011 Malachi and I went from being a family of two to a family of three. I am proud to say, we both like it better with the three of us. After living on our own for years, we met Harry Simmons III. It all started innocently enough, with my now-husband coming to my Manhattan apartment and walking Malachi with me after our dates. Shortly thereafter, Malachi and I were packing our bags and moving to Harry's home in Brooklyn.

It's a big step getting used to a dog being in your house, especially when you did not grow up with pets. Yet Harry stepped up to playing dog daddy with commitment and passion. Malachi was given the run of the house—including access to the couch and bed, and on days when Harry was feeling extra generous, healthy snacks suited to his sensitive stomach. So naturally, when the time came for Harry to propose, Malachi was there.

A year later, Malachi accompanied us again, this time joined by about 200 additional people. We are now an official family of three—Harry, Malachi, and I. Every day I can see how much Malachi relishes the newfound friendship he shares with Harry. My husband is equally able to receive the joy and unconditional love that stems from his four-legged best friend. After days that can be stressful, crazy, and hectic, they both now have each other and a true friendship, in which neither asks for anything in return—except space on the couch.

—Candice Cook Simmons

180

"After days that can be stressful, crazy, and hectic, they both **now have each other** and **a true friendship,** in which neither asks for anything in return— **except space** on the couch.

MASSEY

{ 15+ YEARS ‖ CHIHUAHUA ‖ TEXAS }

Ol' Massey Dog was named after the biggest man I grew up with, Mug Massey, who owned the property next to our farm. He wore overalls every day; smoked, dipped, and chewed at the same time; and died at 83. I thought that this small puppy should have the largest name so he would grow into the rest of our pack, which included a Rottweiler, a black Labrador Retriever, and a Vizsla. Massey was a surprise for my bride that literally fit in the palms of our hands when we got him as a puppy.

Massey has unexpectedly ruled us all. He has the biggest attitude and is the best retriever and highest vertical jumper. He's loyally devoted, highly intelligent, and makes the greatest traveling companion on any form of transportation. He stands, sits, and lies down regally, struts like a Tennessee Walking Horse, is regimented like no other, and is an unbelievable communicator.

Bottom line: Massey is the coolest little dog with a big dog's personality.

—Josh Needleman

WINKY

{ 12 YEARS ‖ BOSTON TERRIER ‖ MASSACHUSETTS }

Winky is the sweetest thing in our life. She has been our constant companion for the past ten years, ever since a friend found her on the side of the road in Houston. She was torn up around the neck and face—apparently from bites—and lost an eye as a result. Even in that first encounter, when she was under so much stress, Winky was gentle and calm. My husband named her for the one eye she had left after the attack.

Winky recently lost her remaining eye after a battle with cataracts and glaucoma, but has continued to do well. She is a cancer survivor who is now mostly deaf as well as blind but still enjoys every day—sniffing around the yard, playing with toys, conniving us into feeding her just what she wants, and coming to work with me.

We are so grateful for the peace and joy that Winky brings into our lives. We cherish spending her golden years with her.

—Daina Bray

SKY 🐾

{ 12 YEARS ‖ AUSTRALIAN SHEPHERD ‖ ALASKA }

Sunshine or snow, hell or high water, Sky likes things to be happening. Her job as an avalanche rescue dog has the sort of intensity that allows her to shine.

We paid for an Australian Shepherd puppy, but Sky turned out to look more like ... well, let's say if she weren't so beautiful she would be "undesirable" to those who might care about a breed standard. But those things are not of the utmost concern for a dog whose job is in the mountains, far from most human eyes, doing difficult work with tremendous style. Always with style.

Sky is older now, still strong but unable to hear much. No time for reminiscing though, it's better to help her remain engaged. Keep things happening. If we work together, maybe, just maybe we can do things with grace. And with style.

—Paul Brusseau

BOOKER

{ 14 YEARS ‖ MIXED BREED ‖ CONNECTICUT }

Booker's eyes never quite fit his body. Even as a puppy, they revealed a surprisingly old soul. He was found in a rough-and-tumble Chicago pound. He was all angles, with his knees and elbows overly pronounced, when we found him, but he grew into a robust, muscular wolf of a dog who could run trails with me at pace. He often galloped the slight ridge above me, only to leap down to my level before the path split. He was all beast.

Over our 13 years together, he has taken in my then girlfriend, now wife; her two cats; and a much younger fox of a dog. He has been a pillow, backyard entertainment, and cleanup crew for our young son. These days, he lies on the blanket beside the newest member of the pack, our daughter.

Booker is our ambassador, our priest, and the perfect companion in the woods. Over the years, he has grayed and grown creaky and even a bit deaf. He has had two knee surgeries, as well as various cancerous growths removed, and is likely not too far from death. I cannot imagine being without him.

Once he's gone, I hope I'll forever call to mind one of the greatest pleasures of our life together: We start atop a hill above Keuka Lake, careen down the dirt path side by side, bristle step across the sharp rock beach, then dash down the dock until we leap, two beasts flying and free, toward the water.

—Matthew Shaw

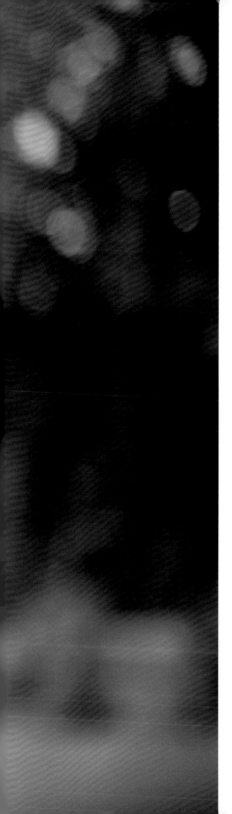

OLIVIA

{ 11+ YEARS ‖ GOLDEN RETRIEVER ‖ VERMONT }

There is a term that describes a very special bond between a dog and its human partners. You may have had many dogs in your life, but only one is connected to you in a way that no other dog has been. This is your "heart dog."

Perhaps it's because Olivia and I have trained together, traveled together, competed together, and visited hospitals, nursing homes, and schools together. Perhaps it's because she has taught me so much more than I could ever teach her. She is kind, patient, loving, so smart, and funny too. She makes me laugh, and someday she will make me cry. She is the best friend, companion, and partner I could have ever imagined.

Olivia is my heart dog.

—Annie Glendenning

COLLAGE CAPTIONS

Page 8 (left to right):
Tara, 7 years (Jim Morrison); Green Dog Rescues, 8–12 years (Colleen Combs); Oliver, 12 years (Kristen Smith); Pablo, 13 years (John Klein); Marley and Sally, both 10–12 years (Jean Davis); Copper, 11 years, and Sam, 10 years (Sandy and Mike Bacino); Johnnie, 14 years (Caroline Kaps)

Page 9 (left to right):
Portia, 11 years (Rocco Maggiotto); Maggie, 15 years (Mara Bovsun); Misha, 13 years (Paula Monteith); Libby, 15 years (Isla Bonifield); Tucker, 15 years (Heidi Chamberlain); Nala, 11 years (Adrien Santarcangelo); Malcolm, 13 years (Jen Heckman)

Page 10 (left to right):
Eden, 15 years (Laurie Branch); Kona, 14 years (Ben Lennon); August, 10 years (Jeannine Armour); Neville, 10 years (Seth Mullen); Bella, 12 years (Julie Busa); Mercury, 16 years, and Ichabod, 15 years (Miriam Cooper); Veda, 13 years (Bidi Dworkin)

Page 11 (left to right):
Coco Pudding, 12 years (Brian and Katy Bailey); Jake, 15 years (Carol Lussky); Ed, 16 years (Joe Miles); Nekia, 10 years (Jennifer Kachnic); Gina, 9 years (Karen Rossbach); Billy, 13 years (Kathleen Colson); Roxy, 10 years (Polly Watson); Muttville Rescues, 10–13 years (Patty Stanton)

Page 196 (left to right):
Moose, 10 years (Dona Tracy); Godiva, 8 years (Bill Hadden); Walter, 10 years (Mary Conway); Ellie, 11 years (Debbie Granquist); Eno, 13 years (Linda McKay); Wisdom, 12 years, and Bliss, 9 years (Leea Foran); Grete, 11 years (Mia Klonsky); Buster, 14 years (Gwyn Dekker)

Page 197 (left to right):
Stella, 15 years (John Maggiotto); Pearl, 12 years (Ken Magoon); Schatzi, 12 years (Roman Scanlon); Betty Davis, 15 years (Joann Alexander); Ginger, 11 years (Julie Renfrow and Nikky Mastro)

Page 198 (left to right):
Mollie, 14 years (Debbie Peretz); Grady, 15 years, and Polly, 11 years (Ally Godinho); Rico, 16 years (Felice Ellis); Ruby, 13 years (Kaki Fisher); Shaggy, 12 years (Tania Gerstenberger); Marcello, 11 years, and Murray, 8 years (Michael Josephs); Dewar, 10 years (Margot Foley)

Page 199 (left to right):
Oak, 11 years (Bill Sweeny); Glory, 13 years (Lu French); Maggie, 13 years (Dawn Kemper); Lily's Legacy Rescues, 12–16 years (Alice Mayn); Sarge, 18 years (Erin O'Brien); Elias, 8 years (Kathy Nimmer); Molly, 11 years (Beth Saradarian)

ORGANIZATIONS

NATIONAL

AMERICAN HUMANE ASSOCIATION
www.americanhumane.org
Animal Welfare Organization

AMERICAN SOCIETY FOR THE
PREVENTION OF CRUELTY
TO ANIMALS (ASPCA)
www.aspca.org
*Animal Rescue and Welfare
Organization*

ASSISTANCE DOGS INTERNATIONAL
www.assistancedogsinternational.org
*Assistance Dog Advocacy
Organization*

BEST FRIENDS ANIMAL SOCIETY
www.bestfriends.org
*Animal Rescue and Welfare
Organization*

BLIND DOG RESCUE ALLIANCE
www.blinddogrescue.org
Dog Rescue Organization

CANINE COMPANIONS FOR
INDEPENDENCE
www.cci.org
Assistance Dog Organization

DOGS ON DEPLOYMENT
www.dogsondeployment.org
Pet Owner Support Organization

THE GREY MUZZLE
ORGANIZATION
www.greymuzzle.org
Funding for Senior Dog Rescue

GUIDING EYES FOR THE BLIND
www.guidingeyes.org
Assistance Dog Organization

INTERNATIONAL ASSOCIATION
OF ANIMAL HOSPICE AND
PALLIATIVE CARE
www.iaahpc.org
Animal Health Organization

LUTHERAN CHURCH CHARITIES K-9
COMFORT DOG MINISTRY

www.lutheranchurchcharities.org
Therapy Dog Organization

NATIONAL MILL DOG RESCUE
www.milldogrescue.org
Dog Rescue and Welfare

PETS OF THE HOMELESS
www.petsofthehomeless.org
Pet Owner Support Organization

PILOTS N PAWS
www.pilotsnpaws.org
Pet Rescue Transport

SEARCH DOG FOUNDATION
www.searchdogfoundation.org
Detection Dog Organization

SUSIE'S SENIOR DOGS
www.susiesseniordogs.com
Senior Dog Rescue Advocacy

THERAPY DOGS INTERNATIONAL
www.tdi-dog.org
Therapy Dog Organization

NORTHEAST

ANIMAL HAVEN
New York, NY
www.animalhavenshelter.org
Animal Rescue Organization

CITY OF ELDERLY LOVE
Philadelphia, PA
www.cityofelderlylove.org
Senior Pet Rescue Organization

**CUMBERLAND COUNTY
   SPCA**
Vineland, NJ
*www.southjerseyregional
   animalshelter.org*
Animal Rescue Organization

**HOUSE WITH A HEART
   SENIOR PET SANCTUARY**
Gaithersburg, MD
www.housewithaheart.com
Senior Pet Rescue Organization

**NORTH SHORE ANIMAL
   LEAGUE AMERICA**
Port Washington, NY
www.animalleague.org
Animal Rescue Organization

**RAISING AID FOR DOGS AT RISK
   (RADAR)**
Lancaster, PA
www.radardogs.org
Funding for Dog Rescue

**RUTLAND COUNTY HUMANE
   SOCIETY** 🐾
Pittsford, VT
www.rchsvt.org
Animal Rescue Organization

**SECOND CHANCE ANIMAL
   CENTER**
Shaftsbury, VT
www.2ndchanceanimalcenter.org
Animal Rescue Organization

SENIOR DOG HAVEN & HOSPICE
Wilmington, DE
www.seniordoghaven.org
Senior Dog Rescue Organization

SOUTHEAST

ANIMAL RESCUE NEW ORLEANS
New Orleans, LA
www.animalrescueneworleans.org
Animal Rescue Organization

FAIRY TAIL ENDINGS, INC.
Sarasota, FL
www.fairytailendings.org
Pet Owner Support Organization

KENTUCKY HUMANE SOCIETY
Louisville, KY
www.kyhumane.org
Animal Rescue Organization

**OLD FRIENDS SENIOR DOG
   SANCTUARY**
Mount Juliet, TN
www.ofsds.org
Senior Dog Rescue Organization

VINTAGE PAWS SANCTUARY
Sarasota, FL
www.vintagepaws.org
Senior Dog Rescue Organization

VIRGINIA BEACH SPCA 🐾
Virginia Beach, VA
www.vbspca.com
Animal Rescue Organization

WASHINGTON HUMANE SOCIETY
Washington, DC
www.washhumane.org
Animal Rescue Organization

MIDWEST

GREAT PLAINS SPCA
Merriam, KS
www.greatplainsspca.org
Animal Rescue Organization

ILLINOIS-WISCONSIN SEARCH
  & RESCUE DOGS 🐾
McHenry, IL
www.illwissardogs.org
Detection Dog Organization

PAWS CHICAGO 🐾
Chicago, IL
www.pawschicago.org
Animal Rescue Organization

ST. LOUIS SENIOR DOG PROJECT
www.stlsdp.org
House Springs, MO
Senior Dog Rescue Organization

SANCTUARY FOR SENIOR DOGS
Cleveland, OH
www.sanctuaryforseniordogs.org
Senior Dog Rescue Organization

SENIOR DOGS 4 SENIORS
Chesterfield, MO
www.seniordogs4seniors.com
Senior Dog Rescue Organization

YOUNG AT HEART SENIOR PET
  ADOPTIONS 🐾
Palatine, IL
www.adoptaseniorpet.com
Senior Pet Rescue Organization

SOUTHWEST

RUBY RANCH PET RESCUE
  & SANCTUARY
Phoenix, AZ
www.rubyranchrescue.org
Animal Rescue Organization

CENTRAL TEXAS DACHSHUND
  RESCUE
Humble, TX
www.ctdr.org
Dog Rescue Organization

WEST

ANIMAL RESCUE FOUNDATION
  (ARF)
Walnut Creek, CA
www.arflife.org
Animal Rescue Organization

AUGUST FOUNDATION FOR
  ALASKA'S RACING DOGS 🐾
Girdwood, AK
www.theaugustfund.com
Dog Rescue Organization

BEST FRIENDS ANIMAL SANCTUARY
Kanab, UT
www.bestfriends.org/sanctuary
Animal Rescue Organization

CALIFORNIA GERMAN SHORT-
  HAIRED POINTER RESCUE
Bonsall, CA
www.gsp-rescue.org
Dog Rescue Organization

CONSERVATION CANINES
Seattle, WA
www.conservationbiology.uw.edu/
  conservation-canines/
Detection Dog Organization

ELDER PAWS SENIOR DOG RESCUE
Fresno, CA
www.elderpawsrescue.org
Senior Dog Rescue Organization

GRAND-PAWS SENIOR SANCTUARY
Acton, CA
www.grandpawsrescue.org
Senior Dog Rescue Organization

GREEN DOG RESCUE PROJECT 🐾
Windsor, CA
www.greendogproject.org
Dog Rescue Organization

HELEN WOODWARD ANIMAL CENTER
Rancho Santa Fe, CA
www.animalcenter.org
Animal Rescue Organization

K9 KOKUA
Waianae, HI
www.k9kokua.org
Dog Rescue and Owner Support
  Organization

LABRADORS AND FRIENDS
  DOG RESCUE
San Diego, CA
www.labradorsandfriends.org
Dog Rescue Organization

LILY'S LEGACY SENIOR
  DOG SANCTUARY 🐾
Petaluma, CA

www.lilyslegacy.org
Senior Dog Rescue Organization

LIONEL'S LEGACY SENIOR
  DOG RESCUE 🐾
San Diego, CA
www.lionelslegacy.org
Senior Dog Rescue Organization

MUTTVILLE SENIOR DOG
  RESCUE 🐾
San Francisco, CA
www.muttville.org
Senior Dog Rescue Organization

OLD DOG HAVEN
Lake Stevens, WA
www.olddoghaven.org
Senior Dog Rescue Organization

PEACE OF MIND DOG RESCUE 🐾
Pacific Grove, CA
www.peaceofminddogrescue.org
Dog Rescue Organization

PETS ARE WONDERFUL SUPPORT
  (PAWS)
San Francisco, CA
www.shanti.org
Dog Owner Support Organization

SAFE HARBOR LAB RESCUE
Golden, CO
www.safeharborlabrescue.org
Dog Rescue Organization

SENIOR DOG RESCUE OF OREGON
Philomath, OR
www.sdroregon.com
Senior Dog Rescue Organization

SLED DOG SANCTUARY 🐾
Talkeetna, AK
www.sleddogsanctuary.com
Dog Rescue Organization

TENDER LOVING CANINES
  ASSISTANCE DOGS 🐾
Solana Beach, CA
www.tenderlovingcanines.org
Assistance Dog Organization

THULANI PROGRAM/GERMAN
  SHEPHERD RESCUE OF NORTHERN
  CALIFORNIA 🐾
Aromas, CA
www.thulanidogs.org
Dog Rescue Organization

ACKNOWLEDGMENTS

Special thanks to my husband, Arthur Klonsky, whose love and support has never wavered. He has always been there, not only pushing me forward and providing clarity when needed, but bringing me sustenance in the form of delicious meals and treats. You are my rock.

To Kacey Klonsky, my amazingly talented daughter, who has been my support and with whom I have had the pleasure of working to expand my project to a series of videos. What a joy it is to watch her blossom into a young woman with a deep soul and boundless creativity, and to share with her my passion for all things dog.

Thank you to the creative and talented people who have helped make this project possible. Zara Vasquez-Evens, an amazing artist, brought her fresh perspective to the project with her bright, eye-catching design, the paw print, and original typeface for the title, *Unconditional*. Chris Crawford, a designer, writer, and idea person, has been with me from the project's inception, when I hadn't yet dreamed of making a book. She has been my alter ego, helping propel me forward. Kaitlin Magoon, who I first met through The Grey Muzzle Organization, enthusiastically came on board with a passion for senior rescues, a brilliance in writing and social media, and a gift for research and planning. Evan Nisenson understood what I was creating even before I did. He believed in me and the project, and started tweeting for me when I didn't even know what a tweet was.

Sarah Foster, my photo editor at Getty Images, has been my objective and brilliant eyes for each step of this process. I can't thank her enough for always generously being there and for helping me see the forest through the trees.

Thanks to my friend Lisa Cueman, the talented photographer, for dropping everything when I needed photos of Charlie, Sam, and me.

Heartfelt thanks to Drew Epstein, my friend and legal counsel for more than 30 years, for his advice and for keeping me grounded; to my very smart friends Brenda Nicholson, Debbie Peretz, Debbie Granquist, Kathy

Fisher, Mary Castner, and Ann Gavett, who provided advice, moral support, and help with editing; and to my friends Ed Morrow, Leslie van Breen, Janet Irving, and Rocco Maggiotto, prominent leaders in the jungles of publishing and business, for helping me wade through it all.

To Lisa Waddle, whose *AKC Family Dog* article, "Older Dogs, Deeper Love," about the project, generated the subtitle we have proudly used for this book.

I am so grateful to everyone who graciously helped connect me with subjects for my photos. Particular thanks to Michelle Brier, Patty Stanton, Marie Macaspac, Jenny Kachnic, Chandra Conway, Dawn Richardson, Laura Oliver, Bob Jachens, Alice Mayn, Holly Turner, Kathy Vayder, Debbie Marks, Dawn Kemper, Diane Wilkerson, Jenni Bidner, Beth Nielsen, and Leea Foran.

I feel fortunate to have friends around the country who supported me with a warm bed, great conversation, and their own dogs to scratch behind the ears when I missed my own: Jean Davis, Wendy Wald, Susan and Michael Josephs, Lynne Taylor, Gwen Bogart, Debbie Moderow, Kathy Nimmer, Mary Jane Murray, Erin O'Brien, and Karen Eisenstadt.

I want to thank my incredibly talented team at National Geographic, who I am proud to say are all women! To Bridget Hamilton, my amazing editor, for believing in me and the project, and pulling together an incredible team. To the team: Moriah Petty, for her hours of editing; Laura Lakeway, my photo editor with an incredible eye; Katie Olsen, whose upbeat design makes me smile. I love you all.

I am deeply indebted to all the people who welcomed me into their homes to photograph them with their dogs. Although this book could only include some of them, each contributed to the project in their own beautiful way. Thank you from the bottom of my heart for sharing your intimate stories with me.

PARTICIPANTS

We'd like to recognize all the other participants who are not pictured in the book but are part of the project. Project Unconditional would not have been what it is today without them.

Oreo & Sue Schiffman
Edie & Dawn Richardson
Tristan & Chelsea Williamson
Kaiden & Debby Dorsett
Laney & Amy Biedron
Shadow and Juno & Nancy Myers
Nicholas & Paulette Blanchard
Doc & Jason Mackey
Lila & Robin Lane
Cleo and Berthie & Glen and
	Linda Hueckel
Buddy & Jan Rogers
Luna & Karen Eisenstadt
Sammy & Kim Ray
Zachary & David Lawrence
Herschel & Maryann Morris
	and Michael Sozek
Winnie & Louise Thanos
Peg & Donna Gates
Rescues & Julie St. Louis
Spencer and Springer
	& Rebecca Knight
Sydney & Sue Allen
Ruby Ranch Rescues & Pam Heine
Clyde & Sandra Coley Greene
Coco & Sia Trujillo
Amika & Carole Kramer
Tess & Connie Bray
Audrey Ann and Minnie Pearl
	& Lee Freilich
Savannah & Rebecca Loehr
Tiny Tim & Susan Ford
Teddy & Jane Lidz
Baltic and Alden & Lena Contreras

Shooter & Lynda and Loren Larsen
Bear and Annie and Nugat
	& Mariane Benetti
Blondie & Marybeth Sobecki
Max & Nicki Avellino
Chipper & Renee Baczynski
Rescues & Jean Kind
Maya & Lynn Miller
Tommy & Jessica Lo
Junie Moon & Wendy Wald
Woody & Blake and Elaine Webster
Kitara & Jim Rabjohn
Jack and Lady & Robert
	and Barbara McLeod
Morrie & Victoria Gelfan
Water Therapy Dogs
	& Louisa Craviotto
Atlas & Dana Medina
Charlie & Gloria Hicks
Lily & Kim Guthke
Gretchen & Lea McComas
Savannah & Jane Calverley
Hope & Nancy LoBalbo
Scooter & Janice Johnston
Olympia & Rich and Dona Martin
Nicky & Ed Tridemy
Crissy & Matt Borkowski and Bill Fride
Izzy and Wrigley & Meg Damato
Quinto & Jenni Bidner
Tater Tot & Jim Pignatari
Sadie & Jen Porter
Twister and Katie & Joyce Paschall
Toby & Andrea Battisti
Amanda & Cheri Trejo

Sammi and Roxy & Ron
	and Lisa Drewniak
Prancer & MaryAnn Hiller
Archie & Rita Wiley
Ginger and Cookie & Sandy Kalemba
Elka & Shirley Kraemer
King & Susan Thomas
Guinan and Maggie Mae
	& Barbara Lax Kranz
Vidalia & Ellen Marshall
Doris & Jamie Carr
Zack & Susan Miller
Sullivan & Terry Cormier
Chelsea & Jim Convery
	and Tracy Craig
Miss Kitty & Lori Olson
Owen and Biscuit & Pamela Gutlon
Coco & Maribel Mendoza
Savannah & Dolores Cimini
Dharma & Mary Thompson
Sanford & Tanya Carujo
Tiro & Rebecca Deperro
Bosco & Gillian Rathbun
Percy & Suzanne Savaria
Shadow & Teresa Cravens
Miriam & Allison Fox
Hershey & Eileen Bottenberg
Lucille and Thea & Katie Michelmore
Ben & Chris Timmins
Dottie & Sandy Snodgrass
Ruby & Garrett Tingum
Magic & Julia Scarbrough and Halle
Libby & Chanda Smith
Brewzer & Chuck Berger

Gracie & Jessie Comba
Crystal & Marilyn Haugen
Snoopy & Bill Aupperlee
Sadie & Bill Hoyt
Tucker & Bob Gasperetti
Bumper & Cynthia Prairie
Sammy & Dana McNair
Sadie & Doris Ingram
Casper, Lucy and Bear & Phillipa
	and Howard Lewis
Tucker & Jessica van Eyck
Spencer and Jenna & Joan Bradley
Wesley & Joyce Pedone
Mac & Kathy Jo Magan
Pia & Linda Drunsic
Julia & Linda Baccki
Red & Lisa Lovering
Toddy & Maynard Deen
Keeta & Mimi Neff
Oakley & Nina Mooney
Ronnie & Ron Pero
Bailey, Polo, and Piper & Ruth Daley
Ella & Conrad Tuerk
	and Ruxana Oosman
Cleo & Ryan Neidhold
Monie & Steve Jones
Tristan & Susan Powers
Jojo & Suzanne Hodges
Boris & Wendy Seier
Mariah & Weslie Porter
Tessa & Alice Gilborn
Polly & Amos Smithwick
Neece & Elise Bartlett
Winnie and Clark & Leslie Miller

Nothing Gives More Meaning to Man's Best Friend Than
TALES OF DOGGY DEVOTION

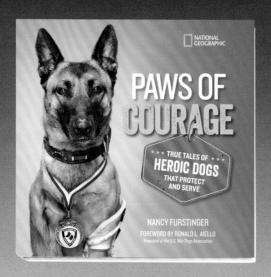

NATIONAL GEOGRAPHIC

PAWS OF COURAGE
★ ★ ★ TRUE TALES OF ★ ★ ★
HEROIC DOGS
THAT PROTECT AND SERVE

NANCY FURSTINGER

FOREWORD BY RONALD L. AIELLO
President of the U.S. War Dogs Association

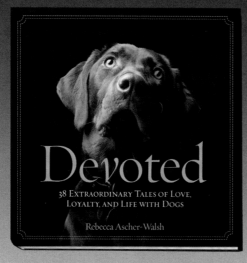

Devoted
38 EXTRAORDINARY TALES OF LOVE,
LOYALTY, AND LIFE WITH DOGS

Rebecca Ascher-Walsh

NATIONAL GEOGRAPHIC

TRUE STORIES OF DOGGIE DEVOTION

PUPPY LOVE

LISA M. GERRY

NATIONAL GEOGRAPHIC